W9-DBG-838

JOBS

By Joanna Brundle

KidHaven
PUBLISHING

A Look at Life Around the World

Published in 2019 by
KidHaven Publishing, an Imprint of Greenhaven Publishing, LLC
353 3rd Avenue
Suite 255
New York, NY 10010

Designer: Jasmine Pointer
Editor: Kirsty Holmes

Photocredits: Abbreviations: l-left, r-right, b-bottom, t-top, c-center, m-middle. All images are courtesy of Shutterstock.com. With thanks to Getty Images, Thinkstock Photo and iStockphoto. Front cover - Tukaram.Karve, wavebreakmedia, Monkey Business Images. 2 - Ververidis Vasilis. 4 - Rawpixel.com. 5 - iMoved Studio. 6 - Roman Yanushevsky. 7t - Shaun Barr. 7b - CLP Media. 8l - thomaschristiawan. 8r - Salvador Aznar. 9t - INDONESIAPIX. 9bl - photo-denver. 9br - P-Kheawtasang. 10t - Dmitry Kalinovsky. 10b - Ondrej Zabransky. 11t - Bufflerump. 11b - kavalenkava. 12 – chrisdorney. 13l - Julia Kuznetsova. 13r - katacarix. 14 – clicksabhi. 15m - Zvonimir AtleticT. 15tr - SOMRERK WITTHAYANANT. 16 – Worldpics. 17 - VanderWolf Images. 18l - Mari_May. 18r - Marco Aprile. 19 - Darlene Munro. 20t - Yuri Turkov. 20b - Leonard Zhukovsky. 21t - Jefferson Bernardes. 21b - Abdul Razak Latif. 22 - 3Dsculptor.

Cataloging-in-Publication Data

Names: Brundle, Joanna.
Title: Jobs / Joanna Brundle.
Description: New York : KidHaven Publishing, 2019. | Series: A look at life around the world | Includes glossary and index.
Identifiers: ISBN 9781534528475 (pbk.) | ISBN 9781534528499 (library bound) | ISBN 9781534528482 (6 pack) | ISBN 9781534528505 (ebook)
Subjects: LCSH: Job hunting--Juvenile literature.
Classification: LCC HF5382.7 B78 2019 | DDC 331.702--dc23

Printed in the United States of America

CPSIA compliance information: Batch #BW19KL: For further information contact Greenhaven Publishing LLC, New York, New York at 1-844-317-7404.

Please visit our website, www.greenhavenpublishing.com. For a free color catalog of all our high-quality books, call toll free 1-844-317-7404 or fax 1-844-317-7405.

CONTENTS

Words that look like this can be found in the glossary on page 23.

ALL KINDS OF JOBS

Every day, millions of people go to work. They might work inside or outside, alone or in a team, traveling or at home. In this book, we will take a trip around the world to find out about the different jobs that they do.

What jobs do you think these people do?

WHY DO PEOPLE HAVE JOBS?

The more these workers pick, the more they are paid.

People work to earn money. They use the money to look after their families and buy things they need. At work, people may help others, be creative, or learn new skills.

WORKING WITH ANIMALS

All around the world, people work as vets, in zoos, in sea life centers, or in wildlife sanctuaries. Some look after dogs or horses. Others work on <u>conservation</u> projects, protecting animals in danger. Some work on farms.

A zookeeper in Israel gets a friendly lick from a giraffe.

ANIMAL HELPERS

China, India, and Australia are important sheep-producing countries. Shepherds use dogs to help them round up the sheep.

Shepherd (UK)

The United States produces more cattle than any other country. Cowboys use horses and a rope called a lasso to round up the animals.

Cowboys in South American countries are called gauchos.

Farmer (U.S.)

WORKING WITH FOOD

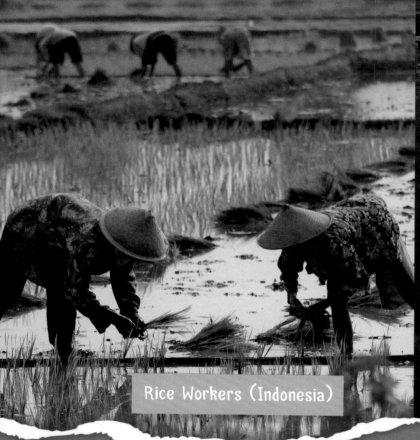

Rice Workers (Indonesia)

Banana Packing (Canary Islands)

People grow, pack, transport, prepare, and cook food. Over a third of the people in the world work growing crops or raising animals for food. People also work in markets, shops, supermarkets, and restaurants. They may sell or serve food.

Do you like chocolate? Let's see what sorts of jobs people do to make it.

1

Cocoa Bean Picking (Indonesia)

2

Chocolate Factory (Belgium)

3

Chocolate Shop (France)

Selling things in shops, also known as retail, provides over one in ten jobs around the world.

JOBS IN TRANSPORTATION

Rickshaw Taxi (India)

Moving people and goods creates lots of jobs on trains, buses, taxis, ships, and ferries.

A rickshaw is also known as a tuk-tuk because of the noise it makes.

Air travel provides jobs for pilots and <u>air traffic controllers</u>. Airports also <u>employ</u> workers in shops, cafes, and restaurants.

Heathrow Airport (UK)

Some places have very famous forms of transportation. New York City is famous for its yellow taxis and their drivers. London is famous for its black cabs. London cab drivers have to pass a special test called "The Knowledge" to prove they know their way around.

Yellow Taxis in New York

Gondoliers make their living working on the canals of Venice, Italy.

JOBS IN TOURISM AND LEISURE

A London Beefeater

Beefeaters work as tour guides at the world-famous Tower of London.

Traveling to new places is called tourism. Many people work in tourism, looking after the needs of travelers. They work in hotels, restaurants, and tourist attractions. Some work as tour guides, showing tourists around.

In cold countries, people work as ski and snowboard instructors. Some work in mountain rescue teams that help people trapped in heavy snow. In sunny countries like Australia, people find work as beach lifeguards.

Lifeguard at Manly Beach, Sydney, Australia

A ski instructor with his pupils in the Alps in Germany

13

WORKING CHILDREN

This boy is collecting plastic bottles at a garbage dump in India.

This boy earns money by selling the bottles for <u>recycling</u>.

Some children do not get the chance to go to school or to play. They have to go to work from an early age. They earn money to help their families. Around the world, about 200 million children work instead of going to school.

This little girl is harvesting corn in Thailand.

This boy is working in a brick factory.

Most child workers are employed on farms. The farms grow crops like coffee, cotton, and rubber. Around 10 percent of child workers are employed in factories. They make clothes, carpets, toys, matches, and cigarettes. Child workers work long hours, earn very little, and their work is often dangerous.

JOBS IN HEALTH CARE

Some people who work in health care work in clean, modern hospitals. Others work without proper equipment and medicine. Volunteers work in places where people have been injured in wars or <u>natural disasters</u>.

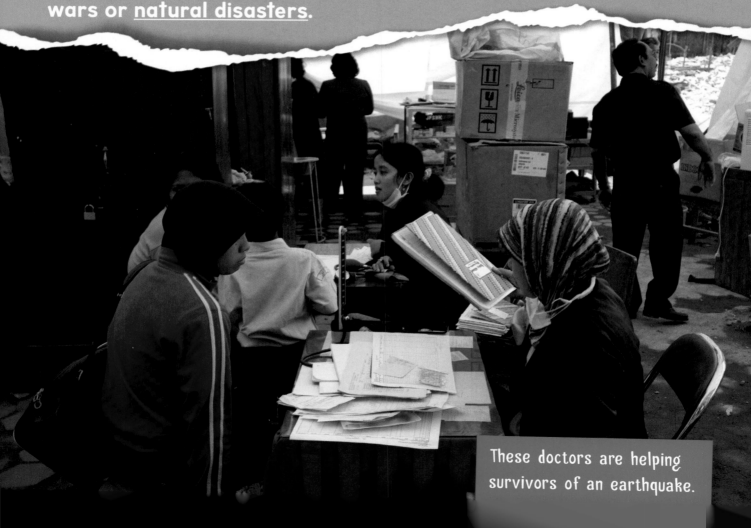

These doctors are helping survivors of an earthquake.

People living in **rural** areas of Australia may have to travel long distances to visit the hospital. The Royal Flying Doctor Service flies doctors directly to these patients. This means people can see a doctor if there is an emergency.

Air Ambulance (Australia)

WORKING IN THE EMERGENCY SERVICES

The emergency services include the police, the fire department, and ambulance services. Trained people work for these services all around the world.

These firefighters in Australia are trying to bring a <u>wildfire</u> under control.

Police Officers (Italy)

The Royal Canadian Mounted Police (RCMP) is the police force of Canada. Officers originally rode horses. Today, horses are used for special events, including the Musical Ride. Officers and their horses take part in performances that raise money for charity.

Officers in the RCMP are called "Mounties."

The bright red uniforms of the RCMP are recognized all over the world.

JOBS IN SPORTS

Wembley Stadium (UK)

Over 5,000 people work at Wembley on match days.

People who play sports for a job are called athletes. Sports also provide jobs in television, and for <u>coaches</u>, umpires, and people working at sports arenas. Television companies employ sports reporters, <u>commentators</u>, and presenters. They also stream live sports all around the world.

Roger Federer

Soccer is played <u>professionally</u> in almost every country in the world.

Formula One drivers are employed to race all over the world, from Australia to Russia, Italy to China. A team of people including mechanics, medical staff, and chefs travel with them.

A team of mechanics work on a car during a race in Malaysia.

A JOB IN SPACE

Some people do a job that is out of this world! Up to six astronauts work on the the International Space Station (ISS). This is a large spacecraft that <u>orbits</u> Earth in space. Astronauts work in space for about six months.

The ISS

Most ISS astronauts have come from the United States and Russia.

GLOSSARY

air traffic controllers	people who direct aircraft on the ground and in the air to prevent accidents
coaches	people whose job is to teach and train a sports team or sports person
commentators	people who describe what is happening at a sporting event
conservation	the protection of things found in nature
employ	to give someone a job
natural disasters	natural events that cause great damage to an area and its people
orbits	travels around a star or planet in space in a regular path
professionally	when someone does something as their job
recycling	reusing materials for different purposes
rural	relating to the countryside
wildfire	a fire in a wild area such as a forest that burns fiercely and out of control

INDEX